Arcola Theatre and the Royal Sh

#WeAreA

by **Can D**

Adapted by **Pippa Hill** & **Sophie Ivatts**
from the English translation by **Feyza Howell**

Son	**Jamie Cameron**
Can	**Peter Hamilton Dyer**
Wife	**Indra Ové**
Supernumeraries	**Jonathon George**
	Harry Reeder
	Jonathan Wober

Director	**Sophie Ivatts**
Designer	**Charlie Cridlan**
Original Lighting Design	**Claire Gerrens**
Re-created Lighting Design	**Laura O'Driscoll**
Sound Designer	**Oliver Soames**
Music Arranger	**Oğuz Kaplangı**
Movement Director	**Ingrid Mackinnon**
Casting Director	**Matthew Dewsbury CDG**
Dramaturg	**Becky Latham**
Magic Consultant	**John Bulleid**
Voice Coach	**Kate Godfrey**
Production Manager	**Julian Cree**
Stage Manager	**Roisin Symes**
Assistant Stage Manager	**Aida Bourdis**
Lighting Programmer	**Michael Paget**
Public Relations	**Chloe Heard** for **Kate Morley PR**
Rehearsal Photographer	**Lidia Crisafulli**
Production Photographer	**Ellie Merridale**
Publicity Videographer	**Laura Clifford**

Commissioned and first produced as part of the
RSC's Mischief Festival at The Other Place in 2018

JAMIE CAMERON
SON

RSC: *#WeAreArrested, Day of the Living, A Midsummer Night's Dream: A Play for the Nation.*

TRAINED: Central School of Speech and Drama, Royal Academy of Music.

THEATRE INCLUDES: *A Christmas Carol* (Old Vic); *Carmen Disruption* (Almeida); *Once The Musical* (original West End cast/Dublin/Seoul).

FILM: *Anna Karenina.*

PETER HAMILTON DYER
CAN

RSC: *#WeAreArrested, A Midsummer Night's Dream: A Play for the Nation, Epicoene.*

TRAINED: Central School of Speech and Drama.

THEATRE INCLUDES: *Twelfth Night, Richard III* (West End/Broadway/Shakespeare's Globe); *King Lear* (Tokyo/Shakespeare's Globe); *The Comedy of Errors, The Tempest, Henry VIII, All's Well That Ends Well, Antony and Cleopatra, The Changeling, The Broken Heart, Anne Boleyn, Gabriel, The Frontline, Holding Fire!, The Golden Ass* (Shakespeare's Globe); *One Flew Over the Cuckoo's Nest* (Nimax UK tour); *The Bacchae* (Shared Experience); *Richard II, The Moonstone* (Manchester Royal Exchange); *Mrs Orwell* (Southwark Playhouse); *The Caretaker, David Copperfield* (Dundee).

TELEVISION INCLUDES: *Downton Abbey, Wolf Hall, Silk, Silent Witness, EastEnders, Holby City, Doctor Who, Waking the Dead, The Bill, Doctors.*

RADIO INCLUDES: BBC Radio Rep, *Scribblers, Bretton Woods, Book of the Week, Ulysses, The Colour of Milk, The Cruel Sea, Mrs Dalloway, The Tempest, Songs and Lamentations.*

INDRA OVÉ
WIFE

RSC: *#WeAreArrested.*

TRAINED: Central School of Speech and Drama.

THEATRE INCLUDES: *The Ugly One* (Park Theatre); *The Interrogation of Sandra Bland* (Bush); *Torn* (Royal Court); *The Curious Incident of the Dog in the Night Time* (Gielgud); *Yes Prime Minister* (UK tour); *Ten Women* (Ovalhouse); *Twelve Angry Women* (Gutted Theatre Co/Lion & Unicorn); *Etta Jenks* (Finborough); *Under One Roof* (Kings Theatre/V&A/Soho Theatre); *Peer Gynt* (Arcola); *The Seagull* (National Theatre Studio); *Blinded by the Sun, A Midsummer Night's Dream* (National Theatre); *900 Oneonta* (Pangloss Productions); *Timon of Athens* (Young Vic).

TELEVISION INCLUDES: *Unforgotten 3, Dark Heart, Flack, Good Omens, Marcella, Requiem, A.D: The Bible Continues, Glue, The Dumping Ground, Topsy and Tim, Casualty, Doctors, The Inbetweeners, Midsomer Murders, Holby City, Best Man, The New Worst Witch, Attachments, Bugs, Space Island One, She's Out, Chandler and Co, Soldier Soldier, The Chief, Desmonds, The Orchid House.*

FILM INCLUDES: *Finding Your Feet*, *Second Spring*, *Jurassic*, *Dubois*, *Still*, *Wonder*, *Mr Invisible*, *Hellhounds*, *My One and Only*, *Blinding Lights*, *Cold Dead Hands*, *Other*, *Club Le Monde*, *It's All About Love*, *Resident Evil*, *Fallen Dreams*, *The Dreamer*, *Cleopatra*, *Cyberstalking*, *Wavelengths*, *More Is Less*, *The Fifth Element*, *Othello*, *Interview with a Vampire*.

RADIO INCLUDES: *Community Flock*, *Madame Butterfly*, *The Wide Sargasso Sea*, *The Audition*.

CREATIVES

JOHN BULLEID
MAGIC CONSULTANT
RSC: *#WeAreArrested.*

John is a Magic Consultant, actor and magician. He holds the title of Associate of the Inner Magic Circle with Silver Star, one of only 268 magicians worldwide with the title.

THEATRE INCLUDES: *Sherlock Holmes: The Final Curtain* (Theatre Royal Bath); *The Invisible Man*, *Partners in Crime* (Queen's, Hornchurch); *Beauty and the Beast* (Watford Palace); *The Star* (Liverpool Everyman); *The Inn at Lydda* (Shakespeare's Globe); *Dirty Dancing* (Secret Cinema); *Dracula* (Paul Ewing Entertainment, Thailand); *The Gypsy Thread* (National Theatre Studio); *The Ladykillers*, *The Secret Adversary* (Watermill Theatre); *Thark* (Park Theatre); *Alice in Wonderland* (Brewhouse Theatre, Taunton); *Murder Most Fowl* (Quay Arts Centre); *A Midsummer Night's Dream* (Theatre in the Forest).

TELEVISION AND FILM INCLUDE: *Coco Report* (Channel 4 News); *You And Universe*, *Loo* (independent short films).

CHARLIE CRIDLAN
DESIGNER
RSC: *#WeAreArrested, Day of the Living.*

THEATRE INCLUDES: Recent work: *Caravan* (Vaults Festival Alias London. People's Choice Award); *Da Native*, *Orator* (Far From the Norm); *Umbra* (Dance Adventures); *Zones*, *Zero For the Young Dudes* (Shell Connections at Soho Theatre); *Mr Stink* (national tour/West End); *Shore* (Riverside Hammersmith); *Brixton Stories* (Lyric Hammersmith/tour); *Lights Out Land Girls*, *Eddie & the Gold Tops* (Bad Apple); *Parkway Dreams*, *Getting Here*, *Cuckoo Teapot* (Eastern Angles).

OPERA INCLUDES: *Wagner Dream* (Barbican); *The Magic Flute* (Peacock Theatre); *Carmen*, *The Pearl Fishers*, *La bohème*, *Jago*, *Eleanor Vale* (Wedmore Opera).

SITE-SPECIFIC: *Uncle Vanya* (Wilton's Music Hall); *Top Dog Live!* (Roundhouse); *The Oresteia Trilogy*, *Don Juan*, *Toad of Toad Hall*, *Around the World in 80 Days*, *The Mother* (The Scoop at More London); *Streets* (Theatre Royal, Stratford East/Roof East/Stratford Circus). *Once upon a Time at the Adelphi* and *Liar's Market* both nominated for Off West End Best Design Awards. Her design for *La bohème* was exhibited at the V&A as part of Transformation & Revelation UK Design for Performance 2007-2011.

OTHER INCLUDES: Designs for Diageo, ?What If! Ltd, The Charles Dickens Museum. She is Designer for Wavelength Connect Ltd.

CAN DÜNDAR
WRITER

RSC: *#WeAreArrested*.

Can Dündar has been working as a journalist for the last forty years, for several newspapers and magazines. He has produced many TV documentaries focusing particularly on modern Turkish history and cultural anthropology. He worked as an anchorman for several news channels. He stepped down from his post as the editor-in-chief of the daily *Cumhuriyet* in August 2016, after he was sentenced to five years and ten months of imprisonment due to his story on the Turkish Intelligence Service's involvement in the Syrian war. He is a columnist for German daily *Die Zeit* and commentator for German WDR's *Cosmo*. He founded the news website called #Özgürüz in exile.

Dündar was nominated as a candidate for the Nobel Peace Prize in 2017. He is the writer of more than forty books, one of which, *We Are Arrested*, was published in England in 2016.

His works were awarded prizes by ten international organisations last year.

CLAIRE GERRENS
LIGHTING DESIGNER

RSC: *#WeAreArrested, The Ant and the Cicada*; *Revolt. She said. Revolt again*. Claire joined the RSC Lighting Department in 2010.

TRAINED: Technical Theatre Arts, RADA.

THEATRE INCLUDES: In Claire's eight years at Stratford she has worked on a number of productions across the Courtyard, RST, Swan, TOP, UK and international tours and transfers, but her highlights so far include: Lighting Re-lighter and Programmer on *A Midsummer Night's Dream: A Play for the Nation*, Lighting Programmer on *The Tempest* (Stratford); Lighting Programmer on *Julius Caesar* (Stratford/ UK and international tour); Lighting Re-lighter on *The Rape of Lucrece* (Stratford/ UK, Ireland and international tour); Lighting Programmer on *Wendy & Peter Pan* (Stratford, 2013 and 2015).

KATE GODFREY
COMPANY VOICE AND TEXT WORK

RSC: Kate is Head of Voice, Text and Actors' Support. *Romeo and Juliet, Macbeth, #WeAreArrested, Day of the Living, Twelfth Night, Julius Caesar, Antony and Cleopatra, Titus Andronicus, Coriolanus, The Tempest, King Lear, Hamlet, Cymbeline, Henry V, King & Country Cycle*.

TRAINED: Central School of Speech & Drama.

THEATRE INCLUDES: Kate was a member of the voice faculty at the Guildhall School of Music and Drama for 20 years and an associate of the National Theatre's voice department since 2001. *One Man Two Guvnors, Dara, 3 Winters, Man and Superman, Three Days in the Country, The Red Lion, War Horse* and the Alan Bennett plays *People*, *The Habit of Art* and *The History Boys* (National Theatre). She has worked on numerous productions in London's West End, and with rep companies such as Chichester Festival Theatre, Manchester Royal Exchange and Sheffield Crucible. She has also coached Japanese actors and directors in Kyoto and Osaka.

FILM INCLUDES: *Callas Forever*, *The December Boys*, *Victor Frankenstein* (with Daniel Radcliffe).

PIPPA HILL
CO-ADAPTOR & DRAMATURG

RSC: *The Boy in the Dress*, *A Museum in Baghdad*, *Crooked Dances*, *Maydays*, *#WeAreArrested*, *Miss Littlewood A Christmas Carol*, *The Earthworks*, *Vice Versa*, *The Hypocrite*, *The Seven Acts of Mercy*, *Fall of the Kingdom*, *Always Orange*, *Queen Anne*, *Don Quixote*, *Hecuba*, *Oppenheimer*, *The Christmas Truce*, *The Roaring Girl*, *The Ant and the Cicada*, *I Can Hear You*, *Wendy & Peter Pan*, *The Empress*, *The Thirteen Midnight Challenges of Angelus Diablo*, *Here Lies Mary Spindler*.

Pippa Hill is Head of Literary at the RSC and oversees the commissioning and development of all of the Company's new plays, adaptations and translations. She also works closely with the creative teams preparing the texts for the classical repertoire. She was previously the Literary Manager at Paines Plough running three nationwide writing initiatives designed to identify and develop new playwrights.

SOPHIE IVATTS
CO-ADAPTOR AND DIRECTOR

RSC: *#WeAreArrested*. **As Associate Director:** *A Midsummer Night's Dream: A Play for the Nation*. **As Assistant Director:** *King John*.

TRAINED: Sophie grew up making amateur theatre, and after studying foreign languages and literature, she trained through various artist development schemes and traineeships, fringe projects and assistant directing. In 2016/17 she was the Clore Fellow for theatre.

THEATRE INCLUDES: As Writer and Director: *I Heart London* (Old Red Lion/ Hen & Chickens, London). As Director: *Live from Frome: A Verbatim Mandate for Art* (Works Canteen, Frome); *The Big Four Oh* (Young Vic Directors); *Got It In One* (Old Red Lion); *It Falls* (Theatre503). As Resident Director: *The Curious Incident of the Dog in the Night-Time* (Gielgud for the National Theatre). As Assistant Director: *Belongings* (Hampstead Theatre Downstairs/Trafalgar Studios); *Cinderella* (Oxford Playhouse).

INGRID MACKINNON
MOVEMENT DIRECTOR

RSC: *#WeAreArrested, Kingdom Come*.

TRAINED: Ingrid holds an MA in Movement: Directing & Teaching from Central School of Speech and Drama.

THEATRE INCLUDES: Ingrid Mackinnon is a London based movement director, choreographer, teacher and dancer. Movement direction credits include: *#DR@ CULA!*, *A Midsummer Night's Dream* (Central School of Speech and Drama); *Fantastic Mr Fox* (associate. Nuffield Southampton/national and international tours); *The Headwrap Diaries* (assistant choreographer. Uchenna Dance/ national tour); *Barbarians* (assistant. Young Vic); *Our Mighty Groove* (rehearsal director. Uchenna Dance). Ingrid is Head of Dance at Wac Arts.

OLIVER SOAMES
SOUND DESIGNER

RSC: Joining the RSC in 2012 as Production Engineer for the national and international tour of *Julius Caesar*, Oliver has since worked as Programmer, Operator and Production Sound Engineer on numerous productions in Stratford. Most recently he redesigned sound for the 2018 tour of *Hamlet* and *#WeAreArrested*.

TRAINED: Birmingham City University.

SOUND DESIGN INCLUDES: *The Situation Room* (Oscar Mike Theatre Ltd); *You: The Player* (Look Left, Look Right); *9* (Co-designer. Chris Goode & Co); *Falling Sickness* (Upstart Theatre); *Country Music* (West Yorkshire Playhouse/tour); *Circo de la Sombre* (West Yorkshire Playhouse).

THE ROYAL SHAKESPEARE COMPANY

The Royal Shakespeare Company creates theatre at its best, made in Stratford-upon-Avon, England, and shared around the world. We produce an inspirational artistic programme each year, setting Shakespeare in context, alongside the work of his contemporaries and today's writers.

Everyone at the RSC – from actors to armourers, musicians to technicians – plays a part in creating the world you see on stage. All our productions begin life at our Stratford workshops and theatres and we bring them to the widest possible audience through our touring, residencies, live broadcasts and online activity. So wherever you experience the RSC, you experience work made in Shakespeare's home town.

We have trained generations of the very best theatre makers and we continue to nurture the talent of the future. We encourage everyone to enjoy a lifelong relationship with Shakespeare and live theatre. We reach 530,000 children and young people annually through our education work, transforming their experiences in the classroom, in performance and online.

THE ROYAL SHAKESPEARE COMPANY

Patron
Her Majesty The Queen

President
His Royal Highness The Prince
of Wales

Chairman
Nigel Hugill

Deputy Chair
Miranda Curtis

Deputy Chair
Baroness McIntosh of Hudnall

Artistic Director
Gregory Doran

Executive Director
Catherine Mallyon

NEW WORK AT THE RSC

We are a contemporary theatre company built on classical rigour. Through an extensive programme of research and development, we resource writers, directors and actors to explore and develop new ideas for our stages, and as part of this we commission playwrights to engage with the muscularity and ambition of the classics and to set Shakespeare's world in the context of our own. We invite writers to spend time with us in our rehearsal rooms, with our actors and creative teams. Alongside developing new plays for all our stages, we invite playwrights to contribute dramaturgically to both our productions of Shakespeare and his contemporaries, as well as our work for, and with, young people. We believe that engaging with living writers and contemporary theatre-makers helps to establish a creative culture within the Company which both inspires new work and creates an ever more urgent sense of enquiry into the classics. Shakespeare was a great innovator and breaker of rules, as well as a bold commentator on the times in which he lived. It is his spirit which informs new work at the RSC. Erica Whyman, Deputy Artistic Director, heads up this strand of the Company's work alongside Pippa Hill as Head of Literary.

Arcola produces daring, high-quality theatre in the heart of East London and beyond.

We commission and premiere exciting, original works alongside rare gems of world drama and bold new productions of classics. Our socially-engaged, international programme champions diversity, challenges the status quo, and attracts over 65,000 people to our building each year. Ticket prices are some of the most affordable in London, and our long-running Pay What You Can scheme ensures there is no financial barrier to accessing the theatre.

**arcola
theatre**

Every year, we offer 26 weeks of free rehearsal space to BAME and refugee artists; our Grimeborn Festival opens up opera with contemporary stagings at affordable prices; and our Participation department creates over 13,500 creative opportunities for the people of Hackney and beyond. Our pioneering environmental initiatives are award-winning, and aim to make Arcola the world's first carbon-neutral theatre.

MAKE THIS HAPPEN — Text **ARCO14 £3** to 70070 to give £3 in support of Arcola Standard network charges apply.

Artistic Director **Mehmet Ergen**	Executive Producer **Leyla Nazli**		Executive Director **Ben Todd**
Assistant Producer **Emma Attwell**	Associate Director **Jack Gamble**	Head of Production **Geoff Hense**	Participation Manager **Bec Martin-Williams**
Events and Operations Manager **Nadja Bering Ovesen**	Producer **Richard Speir**	Front of House & Box Office Manager **Norna Yau**	Front of House & Box Office Assistant Manager / Access Development Manager **James York**
Operations Manager **Natalja Derendiajeva**	Finance Manager **Steve Haygreen**	Chief Technician **Michael Paget**	Finance Assistant **Marcela Rojas**
Office Manager **Jamie-Lee Samuels**	Software Developers **Oliver Brill** **Nick Cripps**	Health & Safety Manager **Charlotte Croft**	New Work Assistant **Eleanor Dawson**
Front of House Supervisors **Emily Jones** **Mary Roubos**	Cleaner **Suber Kemal Sabit**	Participation Assistant Producer **Jordan Turner**	Production Interns **Laura Cliffords** **Olivia Wilkes**

For a full staff list please see **arcolatheatre.com** — *With special thanks to our volunteers and Supporters*

Game Changers
Graham & Christine Benson, Roger Bradburn & Helen Main, Andrew Cripps, Robert Fowler, Daniel Friel, David Alan & Jean Grier, Sarah Morrison, Rosie Schumm

Trailblazers
Katie Bradford, Catrin Evans, Gold Family, Jon Gilmartin, Stuart Honey, Melanie Johnson, Katrin Maeurich

www.arcolatheatre.com — **020 7503 1646**

#WEAREARRESTED

#WEAREARRESTED

By Can Dündar

Adapted for stage by Pippa Hill & Sophie Ivatts
From the English translation by Feyza Howell

OBERON BOOKS
LONDON

WWW.OBERONBOOKS.COM

First published in 2018 as part of *Making Mischief: #We Are Arrested & Day Of The Living* by Oberon Books Ltd.

This single edition published in 2019.

Oberon Books Ltd
521 Caledonian Road, London N7 9RH
Tel: +44 (0) 20 7607 3637 / Fax: +44 (0) 20 7607 3629
e-mail: info@oberonbooks.com
www.oberonbooks.com

PB ISBN: 9781786829047
E ISBN: 9781786829030

Cover image: Ellie Merridale © RSC

Printed and bound by 4EDGE Limited, Hockley, Essex, UK.
eBook conversion by Lapiz Digital Services, India.

Visit www.oberonbooks.com to read more about all our books and to buy them. You will also find features, author interviews and news of any author events, and you can sign up for e-newsletters and be the first to hear about our new releases.

Printed on FSC® accredited paper

10 9 8 7 6 5 4 3 2 1

For Can, Ege and Dilek

Cast

CAN
WIFE / CEO / GRANDMOTHER / MOTHER /
ESTATE AGENT / PSYCHOLOGIST / ENSEMBLE
SON / NEWS EDITOR / PROSECUTOR /
GUL / ENSEMBLE
GUNMAN

Can is pronounced 'Jan'.
When Can speaks, it is direct address to the audience. Speech marks
delineate where he is conjuring up a scene or dialogue from memory.
Gunman watches the play, sitting with the audience.
Neither Can nor the audience should see or acknowledge Gunman
until the end of the play.

(CAN walks onto the stage and greets the audience:)

CAN: Hello.

I used to have a very normal life. I lived with my wife.
And our son. And our dog, Cinammon. I had a lovely
home. A job that I loved. I'd have a glass of wine with
friends after work. Life was good. I didn't realise how
good, until all those things were taken away.

They say the best stories are written facing the most
magnificent views. But I have discovered the opposite to
be true: the imagination, when it meets a wall, can soar to
see what lies beyond.

What follows, in my own words, is a truthful description
of the events that began four years ago and completely
changed my life.

CAN: Thursday, 28 May, 3pm.

An emergency meeting is called on the fifth floor of our national newspaper where I am the editor in chief.

We are here to discuss a video that has been delivered to the paper this morning.

The footage shows a lorry belonging to our National Intelligence Agency being intercepted at the border by armed police.
The police officers search the vehicle. The steel doors open to reveal boxes of medical supplies. But as the police dig deeper, they find heavy artillery underneath: mortar rounds, grenade launchers.

This footage, filmed by the police, is the crucial evidence we need to prove a story we've been investigating for months. It leaves no room for doubt: our country is secretly arming extremists in a foreign civil war. It's one of the biggest stories the paper has ever uncovered. It is a scandal of global proportions.

As a journalist, this is when you ask yourself two questions:
Is this evidence genuine?
Would it be in the public interest to publish it?

If the answer to both is 'Yes', then hiding it in a drawer is a betrayal of your profession. But the stakes are high and there's a general election just days away.

NEWS EDITOR: 'The government has denied involvement in this war over and over again – and now we've got proof they are lying! And not just to us – they are lying publicly to international heads of state! It's against everything this country is meant to stand for. It's clearly in the public interest – we have to publish this'

CEO: 'We can't publish – it's too dangerous. This president is capable of anything.'

NEWS EDITOR: 'Exactly! He's made a major political decision that could change the course of the country's history and he's completely covered it up. The public have no idea, it hasn't even been debated in parliament! People have a right to know before they vote next week!

CEO: *(To CAN.)* 'It has to be your decision. You're the editor in chief – you're the one they'll go after.'

CAN: 'Let's run with it. What's the worst-case scenario?'

CEO: 'If we break the story now, they'll raid the newspaper tonight, seize the papers, and arrest you.'

CAN: 'So let's wait until tomorrow morning to run the story. We'll run teasers on the website, but we won't put the full story online until the morning edition has gone out. That way we minimise the risk of a raid before we publish.'

CEO: 'OK, let's do it. But don't risk getting arrested. Go abroad. Tonight.'

CAN: While I write the leader for the story, my assistant desperately searches for a flight to get me out of the country. There's one seat left on a flight leaving tonight and I think: at least I can visit my son – he is at university there.
Just then, I'm shown a mock-up of tomorrow's front page. It's a still from the video showing all the weapons in the lorry with the headline: 'The Weapons the President Denies'. It is stunning.
I leave the paper and go home in the afternoon, surprising my wife with my early return. The sun is about to set.

We have a glass of wine on the terrace as I give her the news.

CAN: 'I have to leave.'

3

WIFE: 'When?'

CAN: 'Tonight.'

WIFE: 'Do you think the house will be raided?'

CAN: 'I don't think so, but it's not impossible. Don't stay at home tonight.'

WIFE: 'Maybe you shouldn't publish?'

CAN: I don't reply.

I'm at the airport two hours later.

I don't like being away on a night like this. Will the print-run be seized before we can get the papers out?

Will they raid the house, looking for me?

I'm hoping this'll be a brief trip, but could it turn into a long exile instead?

Just then I get a text which puts a smile on my face, in spite of it all. It's from my son.

SON: *My best mate's coming to visit. So happy. The dishes needed doing, Dad!*

CAN: I board the plane at 11pm.

I try to draw on George Orwell for moral support:

'In a time of universal deceit, telling the truth is a revolutionary act.'

CAN: The story explodes overnight.

>   The chief prosecutor launches criminal proceedings
>   against me.
>
>   Our CEO calls me first thing.

CEO: 'It's a ridiculous allegation, but they are trying to get
you on a charge that carries a life sentence. You can't
come back.'

CAN: 'Why? What's the charge?'

CEO: 'Espionage. Revealing state secrets.'

CAN: Espionage?

>   In the middle of this uproar, I meet my son.
>   One single hug, and all the gloom vanishes.
>   We take a long stroll together.
>
>   But my phone never stops ringing, constantly dragging
>   me back to reality. It feels wrong to be standing at a safe
>   distance. But everyone back home is telling me to stay
>   away.
>
>   Then on 31 May during supper with my son, I receive a
>   text from our CEO.

CEO: ***The President's threatening you on national TV. He says:
The journalist who wrote this has betrayed our country. I'll
make him pay a heavy price. I won't let him get away with it.***

CAN: I read the text out to my son.

>   'How should we respond?'

SON: 'Defiantly.'

CAN: I compose a tweet, throwing the president's words back
at him:

*The person who committed this crime will pay the price.
We won't let him get away with it.*

The next day the morning edition of the paper arrives by email. My entire editorial staff have issued a defiant headline –

CEO: *'Journalists – Guilty as Charged'*

CAN: – with headshots of every single one of them on the front page.

I can't stay any longer – I have to stand by them.
I book a ticket for the next flight home.
I say good-bye to my son and I give him a copy of the entire contents of my laptop for safekeeping. I'm setting off into the unknown.
'What message shall I give your mother?'

SON: 'Tell her I'm proud of my dad.'

CAN: The enormity of what we've done sinks in when I board the plane home. The other passengers cheer, shake my hand, give me high fives. I read about myself in the headlines.
I ask myself if I'm afraid. But I know that fear breeds silence.
I step off the plane at the airport of my home town and walk up to the immigration desk. The officer looks first at my passport, then at my face… He smiles, stamps my passport and waves me through.

CAN: The police raid I expect at any moment never materializes. The general election that week brings new hope. The public, gagged in the street, have spoken at the ballot box and deliver a hung parliament. The president's party struggle to form a coalition government, and we are relieved that, for now at least, they are distracted.

Our newspaper is showered with international awards for courageous journalism. But the attention these awards bring makes it increasingly dangerous to publish our stories.
Friends and family are pressing me to buy a gun, to get a bodyguard or a bulletproof car.
In July the police arrest a suicide bomber carrying the address of our office in his pocket.

That summer, I travel abroad to collect our awards.

At one of the award ceremonies, Reporters Without Borders reason with me:

ENSEMBLE: 'We're worried about you. If you stay here with us, we can help you. Don't go back.'

CAN: For many years I've heard tales of exile, and even covered some in documentaries I've made. Most are unhappy stories; homesickness debilitates many and has even killed a few.

I can't accept being made to flee like a criminal.

Back at home, my own country is on fire. All summer, suicide bombers flood our city squares with blood.
In the grip of this nightmare the president holds a blunt knife at the throat of society and whispers, 'Vote for me, and this will stop.'

The president calls a snap general election in November. His party polls five million new votes. It is a landslide.

As we watch the early results come in on the night of the election, no one in the office says a word.

We are weary and unarmed.

My son phones. He's glued to his T.V. screen:

SON: 'It's heart-breaking to watch our homeland slip away like this.'

CAN: My mother rings: she knows my phone is tapped and chooses her words carefully:

MOTHER: 'You know I'd never ask why if anyone wanted to live elsewhere…'

CAN: As we prepare the front page at work that night my Assistant Editor whispers,

NEWS EDITOR: 'I think you should leave tonight. Out of the country. They'll come for you now. They'll come for you in the morning.'

CAN: The fear is palpable.

I get home to my wife in the early hours.

WIFE: 'You should leave.'

CAN: 'I've done nothing wrong.'

This is the moment the idea that I might actually go to prison becomes a real possibility.

We've had our awards. Now it's time for our punishment.

CAN: *'Someone must have been telling lies about Josef K., for one morning, without having done anything wrong, he was arrested.'* That's how Kafka starts *The Trial.*

That's what I'm thinking about on the morning of Tuesday 24th November, when I find the phone on my office desk flashing with a new voicemail:

ENSEMBLE: ***The Chief Prosecutor has summoned you to give a statement at 11am on Thursday, 26 November.***

CAN: The president has just approved his new cabinet and the message on my answerphone is the first act of his new government.

We gather in the big meeting room on fifth floor at 3.45. Our CEO bursts in.

CEO: 'The allegations against you are astonishing! Obtaining and disclosing confidential state documents with the purpose of political or military espionage and aiding and abetting an armed terrorist organisation.'

CAN: 'Aiding a terrorist organisation? Who would believe we're spies; let alone terrorists?'

NEWS EDITOR: 'No one! It's ludicrous!'

CEO: 'You can't put anything past this president.'

CAN: 'OK, so give me the best and worst-case scenarios?'

CEO: 'Best case is they release you on bail, with a ban on foreign travel. But because the charges relate to national security, the risk of a pre-trial detention is pretty high.'

CAN: 'How long do you think they could hold me for?'

CEO: 'A year? Three years? Who knows? You should leave the country. The law's no longer impartial. The courts are all under government control. No one who goes in comes out.'

NEWS EDITOR: 'You won't go to prison! The president has just admitted it on national TV – he's just verified our story! You can't be convicted for revealing an open secret.'

CEO: 'You're wrong. They'll set you up with fake evidence, linking you to terrorism. Then they'll delay a proper trial and put you in prison indefinitely. Under this government, it would actually be better to get you a conviction, so that we can appeal to the Constitutional Court or the European Court of Human Rights.'

CAN: Truly Kafkaesque…

I decide that I will go and offer my statement to the chief prosecutor, come what may.

The following evening after work a large crowd of us stroll over to our favourite local restaurant. We laugh and chat and drink.

We raise our glasses to all our friends at that table. We all wonder if it might be the last drink we'll have together for a long time.

That night at home, I choose the books I want to take to prison, just in case. My wife and I avoid discussing it. We know hard times are ahead. But we do believe we will overcome. This too will pass.
The following day is 26 November.
We will be celebrating our twenty-eighth wedding anniversary.

CAN: When I was a child, my grandmother always started with a kindly,

GRANDMOTHER: 'Oh,'

CAN: /and

GRANDMOTHER: 'God is great, son,'

CAN: No matter what the topic was, how important or trivial.

Her unshakeable belief would make you assume that no evil deed would ever be left unpunished and that no injustice would prevail upon the earth.

GRANDMOTHER: 'God is great!'

CAN: /consoles the victim and threatens revenge upon the vain.

She would stroke my face and say,

GRANDMOTHER: 'God is great,'

CAN: And I would be comforted. But as I grew up, I had questions:

'If he's that great, why doesn't he break thieving hands? Why doesn't he return my marbles and punish the kid who stole them? Why does he withhold his mercy?'

Whenever I asked these questions, she would shush me with a,

GRANDMOTHER: 'Repent!'

CAN: /and shelter in the only justice she trusted:

GRANDMOTHER: 'God is great!'

CAN: I ring my mother on the morning I'm due in court.

MOTHER: 'God is great, son,'

CAN: /she says.

It's raining.
I put on my smartest velvet jacket and my favourite shirt.
Suitable for defeat or celebration.

The Justice Palace is filled with friendly faces: writers,
journalists, MPs, and my colleagues. I'm alarmed to learn
that Gul, the head of our regional office, has also been
summoned.
I give a short statement at the door:

'We're not spies, traitors or heroes; we're simply
journalists. We're here to defend journalism and the
public's right to be informed. We won't be intimidated.
We will stand up and defend our words.'

Gul and I are interviewed separately.

I step into the prosecutor's office at 11.20.
The prosecutor is cheerful and impeccably courteous.

As we sip our teas, he points to the thick blue folders on
the filing cabinet.
They contain a 10,000-page report on the activities of
the political pressure group we are accused of colluding
with. A group the president now describes as a terrorist
organisation.

I'm curious to see how on earth he'd connect them with
me.
It seems I aided and abetted the group 'unwittingly.'

PROSECUTOR: 'You have divulged state secrets.'

CAN: 'So it is true then: the government are shipping arms
and it's a state secret.'

PROSECUTOR: 'Whose right is it to decide what can be known, and what cannot be known? The government's, of course.'

CAN: 'And what if the government were committing a crime? What if that crime was concealed under the label of "state secret"? Who would monitor that? The National Intelligence Agency was acting beyond its legal authority. They were smuggling weapons illegally for a war which we had no democratic mandate to involve ourselves in – and absolutely no transparency about who those weapons were intended for. And the government lied about it: to us and to the rest of the world.

It is a journalist's duty to expose any crime – regardless of who the perpetrator is.

A journalist is not a civil servant.'

PROSECUTOR: 'And do you think an intelligence agency can admit that it's shipping weapons?'

CAN: 'Of course not. But neither could any journalist ignore it.'

PROSECUTOR: 'So you think anything could be news then? You know about the German Chancellor's naked photos taken when she was very young? The German papers didn't publish them. Would you publish my naked photo if you found it? Are there no limits?'

CAN: 'Public interest defines the limits. There's absolutely no public benefit to publishing naked photos of Angela Merkel – or you! But it is in the public interest to know if the state is committing a crime.'

Several cups of tea later, the prosecutor still doesn't look convinced.

PROSECUTOR: 'The interception of that lorry was a trap set for our country. A trap set by a rogue terrorist group.'

CAN: 'And we belong to that group do we?'

PROSECUTOR: 'We'll be laughed out of court if we try to claim that.'

CAN: 'Sir, this group you are suddenly so anxious about is an organisation our newspaper has consistently investigated and openly criticized for years. Surely the government cannot accuse us of colluding with them? Where's your evidence?'

PROSECUTOR: 'Is this your telephone number?'

CAN: 'Yes.'

PROSECUTOR: 'Did it belong to you between 20th and 30th May?'

CAN: 'Yes.'

PROSECUTOR: 'Do you know these two people or recognise their phone numbers?'

CAN: 'No.'

PROSECUTOR: 'They were recorded exchanging messages on 28th May discussing the publication of your report. Are you aware of this exchange?'

CAN: 'No.'

PROSECUTOR: 'OK. That will be all.'

CAN: 'Really? That's your evidence? No fake telephone conversations? No faked money transfers into hidden bank accounts? Are you seriously planning to arrest me on an allegation of espionage based on a Twitter exchange between two people I've never heard of?'

They have nothing.
Not a shred of evidence.

Gul and I both emerge smiling from our interviews.

'They've got no case against us,' we tell friends waiting at the door.

We sit down on the floor with our friends and lunch on toasted sandwiches and yoghurt drinks.

Suddenly a clerk emerges.

ENSEMBLE: 'You are both summoned to court for arrest.'

CAN: A cloud of bewilderment sweeps through the hallways.
How can this be happening?
My telephone is ringing non-stop.
Voices of outrage rail from all quarters.
I compose a Tweet:
We are arrested.
But I stop short of sending it.

We walk into the highest court in the land and our statements from the prosecutor's office are read out to the judge. He then announces our arrest, speaking for about ten seconds before he leaves the courtroom.
I hear a yell from somewhere behind:

ENSEMBLE: 'Shame on you!'

CAN: I hit 'Tweet': *We are arrested*.
The courtroom is in uproar.
I embrace my wife and whisper 'Happy anniversary.'

CAN: Six or seven anti-terror squad officers escort me and
Gul down to the car park.

We say our goodbyes.

We set off, down the road I walk daily on my way to the
newspaper.

Familiar buildings, shops, pavements and people all sweep
past the car windows. It all looks different tonight.

For the first time in my life, I try to carve familiar images
into my mind. I don't know when I'll see them again.

An hour and a half later, the prison appears on the
horizon. We cross beyond the prison wall at midnight.
The soil ends.

This is a land of concrete and iron. Walls and barbed wire
everywhere.

How long can they actually keep us here? It is impossible
to believe we are to be held in such a high security prison
without even having been to trial.

We stop at the last courtyard and get out of the car.

A vast iron door opens.

We step in. Gul is taken away as we are led to our cells.

Now the key.

Then the bolt.

And finally the screw iron handle.

My solitary confinement begins.

CAN: Can you go back a century in one step? Tonight I have. Alone in a cell in prison.

None of the objects that have entered our lives in the last century are here.

No mobile phones or computers, no Internet.
No washing machine, dishwasher or fridge.
No TV, radio, or table lamp.
Not even a rug, curtain, armchair or teapot.

They are going for a minimalist look. I take in the cell like a flat-seeker, unconvinced by the offerings of a pushy Estate Agent:

ESTATE AGENT: 'A white plastic table. A white plastic chair. Three iron beds. One kitchen worktop. A steel cupboard on the worktop. Surprisingly spacious. A two-story villa of 25 square metres. A seven-pace by seven-pace room downstairs.

There's a walk-in shower room with toilet. Another brown iron door opposite the entrance opens to the courtyard; although, sadly, it is locked at this time.'

CAN: The room and I stare at each other.

My black velvet jacket looks the white plastic chair up and down, as if to say, 'I must have got the wrong wedding.'

I open the toilet door: as tiny and squalid as one you'd find in a petrol station. The shower is a step away from the squat toilet. And the washbasin, another step away.

There's a mirror taped to the wall.
A two-inch gap between the iron door and the floor, and I can smell sewage.
The stairs lead up to three battered old beds, bolted to the floor.
'Thankfully I won't be staying long,' I think.

Then laugh at myself.

Everything echoes here.
Steel pipes gush like a waterfall, an iron door slams like a thunderclap.
I switch off the fluorescent light.
The floodlight from the yard falls into the room, diced into a grid by the window bars that cast faint shadows on the beige floor tiles.
It looks like moonlight in the darkness.

CAN: Next morning, I'm still rubbing my eyes when four silhouettes in navy blue uniforms climb upstairs, look at me and leave, unlocking the door to the yard as they go.

Now the cell looks like a concrete matchbox, with its tray pushed out.

I step out into the yard. It's a sunless, soilless and flowerless garden enclosed by a ten-metre high wall rising to cloudy skies, wearing a crown of barbed wire. The familiar, vast, bright blue countenance of the sky is hemmed in between these wires. I inhale that handful of sky.
Every eight paces, you meet a wall.

Gul has to be beyond the wall, but it's impossible to hear or see him.

I'm just thinking I could do with a cup of tea, when I hear a noise. Something drops into the yard.

(A red apple flies over the wall.)

Three bright red apples!

I'm staring up into the air, trying to work out which direction it has come from, when a second parcel flies over the barbed wire.

(A bottle full of tea flies in.)

A plastic soda bottle wrapped in newsprint. And inside… Yes! Piping hot tea, with some sugar cubes too.

ENSEMBLE: 'Welcome.'

CAN: 'Thank you. Thank you; who are you?'

He tells me his name, but I can't make it out. The wall breaks up the sound.

ENSEMBLE: 'Speak through the grate.'

CAN: I realise it's the Editor-in-Chief of another newspaper. He and his deputy were brought to the prison a month before Gul and me.

ENSEMBLE: 'The papers have covered your arrest in great detail. Massive outrage. I heard protest marches would take place today.'

CAN: 'Thank you, Thank you, wonderful news!'
Immediately, I feel less alone.
I save one of the apples and try to lob the other two to Gul in the same way.
In vain. My parcel doesn't clear the barbed wire.
As I practise my catapulting technique, a final gift arrives from the other wall:

(A newspaper flies in.)

It is today's edition of the paper. Now that is a miracle. *'Media's Black Day'* is the headline with a photo of my wife and I at the courthouse yesterday. I wonder how many of the other papers have dared to report the story.

Just then the heavy iron hatch of the cell door opens and a piece of paper appears,
(A form appears.)

ENSEMBLE: 'Canteen price list. Choose what you want off the list. You can spend up to 50 per week'.

CAN: 'How do I get money?'

ENSEMBLE: 'Ask your visitors to deposit it.'

CAN: 'Can I have newspapers and a T.V.?'

ENSEMBLE: 'Request them on these forms.'

CAN: And he hands me a biro and a yellow notepad and shuts the hatch.

(A yellow notepad and a pen appear.)

I turn the order forms over – they are blank on the back.
He has just given me the world.
Pen and paper…
My two oldest friends are now with me.

CAN: Dear Friend,

Here we are again, together.

Whenever I'm in trouble, you're the first one to take my arm.

We've travelled so far together…

You have been my comrade, my confidant, my everything, since that first day I put pen to paper.

You it was who found my first love, and my last.

You it was who paid the first instalment on my first bookcase, and the mortgage on my house.

You have fed me for years and years, paid me a salary.

And now we're here, locked up together…

And you're going to reach out and grab me by the hand.

You will laugh and cry with me.

You will write my solace and my defence.

You put me in this cell and you will get me out.

You will put me on a paper plane and fly me off to the next yard, to the world beyond the wire and walls, to freedom, and my loved ones.

(During this speech, CAN rips a piece of paper from the yellow notepad and creates a paper aeroplane.)

CAN: Any detainee who wants to see a psychologist can.

I say yes out of curiosity.

They lead me to a room where I sit down facing a young interviewer. She is impeccably polite.

PSYCHOLOGIST: 'Your name please?

And your age?'

And your profession please?'

And are you here on terror or criminal charges?'

CAN: 'I'm a spy.'

I say it as if I'm James Bond.

'I'm accused of espionage but, it seems I'm a bit of a novice. I splashed the first bit of information I got all over the front page of a newspaper, instead of passing it on to the secret service. I got caught on my very first mission. And I've been locked up so I can't tamper with the evidence.'

PSYCHOLOGIST: 'Who introduced you to crime?'

CAN: 'My mother. You see, when I was still a baby, she read me books and that way she prepared me for crime. Then there was my primary school teacher. By teaching me to write, she had equipped me with the instrument of crime.'

PSYCHOLOGIST: 'Are you going to continue to commit crimes after your release?'

CAN: 'So it seems. I can't stop reading or writing.'

We end the interview.

CAN: The iron hatch in the door opens. A voice calls in:
'Solicitor to see you.'
Or, 'MP visit.'

Every time I leave the cell I am subjected to a body search…
Remove shoes, right one first… Bang the heel on the floor, and put it back on. Then the left… Bang the heel on the floor, and put it back on. Walk. Take sixty steps. Halt.

The Visit Room is like an aquarium. Glass cubicles are arranged in a row like a train with a glass divide between inmate and visitor. Handsets to talk through.
In this fish-tank, I entertain over 200 lawyers and politicians during my detention.

CAN: My wife visits.

I'm taken from my cell. Body search. Walk. Take sixty steps. Halt. Repeat.

I'm bursting with excitement.

We leap up as if we haven't seen each other for months. We are separated by the thick panel of glass. Our palms kiss on either side of the window; the kiss of our fingers leaves their mark on the glass.
She looks so elegant, strong and determined. She is cheerful and brave. The magnificent firebrand I fell for as a student resurfaces at times of crisis and is born again.
Earlier today, she addressed the crowds outside the newspaper:

WIFE: 'We are deeply proud of this paper's integrity and its ongoing fight against oppression.'

CAN: She gives me all the news.

WIFE: 'Our mothers have both been in tears. I've consoled countless callers who ring the house. I tell them to channel their feelings into action.'

CAN: There is a moment when we both realise that in prison there is nothing more to hide. So we enjoy this new openness and feel free to poke fun.

'I'll grow my beard until I'm acquitted if that's all right with you,'.

WIFE: 'Any excuse.'

CAN: 'You've never much liked a beard on me.'

WIFE: 'I've brought you your books, and a few of my favourites too.'

CAN: The handset beeps to tell us that the hour has gone. Time's up.
I show her the tiny passport photo I've hidden in my pocket.
A photo taken in a tiny cubicle

WIFE: Not much different to this one, our son between the two of us. A photo full of wide grins.

CAN: She looks; her eyes fill. We gaze at each other.
The line is cut.

Back in my cell, the TV set arrives.
I watch footage of the protests against our arrest.
'You're not alone!' yell the banners in the streets.
It is as if a twenty-nine-channel spaceship has landed in the medieval décor, brightening up the dark cell with the warm glow of solidarity

CAN: The paper regularly try to send me a press digest, so I know what's going on in the outside world. I am used to our pro-government press inventing stories about me – I have come to expect it.

Today, one of their tabloids runs a slur that claims I'm hiding my son's true parentage:

ENSEMBLE: *Liberal Journalist's Illicit Love-child. What else is he lying to us about?*

'The whinging journalist claims he was arrested on his 28th wedding anniversary. Official records show that he married in 1991 but that his son was born in 1989... is he another man's son? For someone so obsessed with telling the truth, is this man really a liar?'

CAN: And so on. More of the same alternative facts that have gradually, somehow, become normal.
I usually ignore it, laugh even. But today, I suffer a total sense of humour failure.
I am livid.
Perhaps it's because of the depravity of kicking someone when they're down.
Perhaps, because the truth is that our son was a blessing after three heartbreaks.
But what can I do?
I can't send in a correction request. I can't make them stop.
I hurl obscenities at the walls, the heavens and the city...
I shock myself with my own fury.
I've never seen myself like this.

It passes. I distract myself.
And I forget it a few hours later.

Then it's announced on TV that the journalist behind the article has died suddenly of a heart attack. As though it is

26

my curse that has killed him. I'm suddenly scared by the power of my rage.

I forget the slurs the dead man has written about us and address the heavens:
'God forgive his sins. Don't let me come out of here full of vengeance.'

Just then my grandmother whispers into my ear,

GRANDMOTHER: 'God is great, son.'

CAN: Outside, the weekend is a welcome break.

Inside, it's the opposite...

The prison goes to sleep on Saturdays and Sundays.

Time, that gushes like a waterfall on visit days, trickles like still waters once the week is over.

The voices fall silent, the canteen is shut.

The gloom of a deserted public office settles into the corridors.

As the weeks pass my sense of time becomes colonised.

Telephone day.

Visitors' day.

Exercise day.

Post day.

These routines are designed to quietly convict you. The aim is to turn me into a lifer before I've even been tried.

You become a prisoner to waiting.

The cell is a waiting room:

You wait for the papers to come, for the bread, for the yard door to be unlocked, for the meal, for the evening, for a match on TV, for night, for morning.

But most of all, for release.

But on my first Saturday in prison, I'm naive and willful.

I resolve to break the routine imposed upon me.

My first act of rebellion is to target monotony.

I discover that the charmless toilet-cum-shower can be transformed into a steam room if I run the hot water for a couple of minutes – and use my imagination. And the bare walls become a magnificent backdrop for performing songs in the shower.

The breakfast scheduled for 0800 can wait.

I decide that I would rather brunch instead.

But the venue looks a bit dull.

I decide I will eat 'al fresco'.

I carry the white plastic table to the yard, deploy the duvet cover as a tablecloth. I put on my jumper and jacket. I fold the blanket into a cushion for the plastic chair.

I will transform this tasteless food into a sumptious feast.

(A beautiful hotel room service tray appears. On it is a silver cloche, a coffee cup and a carafe of water. CAN takes each item and places it on the prison table. A glass of Buck's Fizz appears from out of his copy of 'War and Peace' which is on the table, the coffee cup fills with freshly brewed coffee, and the cloche yields a stale piece of bread. CAN replaces the cloche and opens it again to reveal a plate of delicious pastries, cakes and croissants.)

There's still something missing.
Of course! Music!
I pull the TV set as close to the yard window as I can, find the music channel and turn the volume all the way up.
The empty yard amplifies the music.
The whole prison reverberates with the sound.
I take a break from brunch and dance to Adele's *Hello.*

(CAN's wife appears here. He creates a rose out of his red napkin and gives it to her. They dance with conspiratorial joy. She leaves. He is devastated.)

CAN: Gunshots rouse me from a peaceful siesta.

The TV screen is awash with blood.

ENSEMBLE: *A prominent lawyer and civil rights activist has been shot dead today. He was shot once in the head by an unidentified gunman. He was making a statement to the press, calling for an end to the violence between the government and minority activist groups.*

CAN: In his final tweet, he'd written about Gul and me:

ENSEMBLE: ***Their arrest is the greatest blow yet to freedom of press and expression. Without any social resistance, we'll soon find ourselves beyond the point of no return.***

I fling myself out into the concrete garden. I start pacing in an oval formation in the rectangular yard. Coming up against the same wall at each corner, I pace in the cold.

One-two-three-four-turn...

One-two-three-four-five-six-seven-eight-turn...

One-two-three-four-turn...

One-two-three-four-five-six-seven-eight-turn.

CAN: The hatch opens.

ENSEMBLE: 'Letter for you.'

CAN: It is placed into my palm like a white dove bearing glad tidings.

The writing on the envelope is a familiar scrawl.

I take it and go upstairs. Stretch out on a bed.

SON: *Dear Dad,*

I thought I'd write a letter, but did wonder if my terrible handwriting might push you over the edge in the middle of all your troubles. Not to mention the spelling mistakes! Please forgive me.

What a strange world this is. Someone has drawn walls and wires between us.

I can't hide how much I miss you... 'Don't worry,' I tell myself, he'll turn up in the fresh light of some morning, maybe in the winter, maybe in the spring, maybe in the middle of his favourite season... We'll eat Nutella from the jar again, watch a match, maybe even take a road trip up Highway 61 in an old Cadillac, BB King belting out 'Thrill is gone!' as we race off into the sunset, like two cowboys...

Don't worry... I know you won't, but never lose hope. The future is on our side. The greatest privilege of my life has been knowing your hands were holding the back of my bike in every adventure I set off on. Neither walls nor death can separate us. You're with me every day.

Read and write. Keep taking the piss out of everything and defy the days they've laid out in front of you.

Dad, I am proud to be your son and honoured to be your friend. I can't wait for the day when we'll meet again.

I kiss your hands and eyes.
Your son.

CAN: A very dear friend once gave me some advice:

Don't be ashamed to bend if you're punched. If you insist on standing straight, your internal organs might be damaged. Best to just buckle under the pain and straighten up later.

I take that advice today. I let go of the lump I'd been harbouring in my throat for months, and I buckle. I sob and sob in an unscheduled resistance break.

CAN: Nothing smells here.

> The campus is so thoroughly surrounded by concrete,
> iron, wall and mortar that not even odours can penetrate.
> No comforting aromas of food, or soil, flowers, or sweat or
> perfume. Only sewage.

> It is in one of the early weeks when a letter breaches this
> blockade and a scent rises up off the paper like incense.

WIFE: *I thought this scent would suit you: Agent Provocateur.*

CAN: Only too true. Outside, the pro-government press
campaign is intensifying against me. This week they brand
me as an 'enemy agent' and a 'traitor'.

> I drink in the scent and smile.

CAN: One of our most respected colleagues, a veteran journalist, arrives at the prison gate at 8.30 on the cold morning of the 2nd of December, carrying a wooden chair. He places it on the ground, sits down and announces the beginning of the Vigil of Hope.

ENSEMBLE: 'I'll stay here for a day. If each of us keeps this vigil for one day, this will turn into a chain. Today I'm the first link in this chain.'

CAN: His one-man protest finds support straight away. The Press Council are inundated with offers of support from journalists and organise them into a rota. Coach-loads come from all across the country to join the protest at the prison gate. Old folk songs drift over the walls, they hold kite festivals and concerts. In the coldest days of winter, come wind, rain or snow, the wooden chair draws crowds to the prison gate; we receive their messages, hear their voices and we feel less alone.

On 12th December, our news coordinator at the paper has an inspirational idea. He brings our weekly editorial staff meeting to the prison gate. My colleagues discuss the agenda wrapped up in their coats in the cold winter's air. Then he visits me and asks for the headline.

It's a symbolic act and it captures the imagination of the worldwide press.

CAN: Prison has quite a long list of bans.

Rugs, curtains and heaters are forbidden.

Wearing a tracksuit to a legal visit is forbidden, as are hanging anything on the walls, placing a lamp on the table, or using a typewriter.

Soil or potted plants in the cell are forbidden.

Reading a book during transport or chatting with the other prisoners is forbidden.

One of the things I miss most is colour.

Even coloured pens are forbidden.

But where people live, there will be colour.

I put the address of the prison at the bottom of the columns I smuggle out to the paper, and add:

Anyone who wants to write to me is welcome.

The moment friends and family hear about the colour ban, they post colourful envelopes and sheets and pads of paper.

One friend sends in a couple of fleeces, one turquoise and the other orange.

A reader sends in nature photographs; I festoon the grey worktop with grass, flowers and trees.

The more you are restricted, the more determined you become to break free.

I learn how to make colour.

I stick coloured newsprint onto steamed glass and scrape off the dripping ink using a razor blade.

First, I distill yellow ink from the coat of a society bride and I paint a daisy.

Then I dip into the red jacket of a jet-set crown prince to paint a rose.

I feel like a Robin Hood stealing colours from the rich for his humble abode.

Not satisfied, I attack the fruit next.

Dipping my toothbrush into orange scraped from orange peel, burgundy from radishes and green from apples, I paint. That's how I overcome the colour ban.

CAN: At the end of December snow sprinkles like confetti over the rooftops, dancing in the prison searchlights…

I watch from the window: the snowflakes shove and push each other. When they land singly on the stones, they melt and vanish.

But while we are sleeping, the snowflakes realise that when they stop scuffling with each other and unite, it snows hard enough to cover the yard.

When I wake on 29 December, the snow is laid out like a spotless sheet.

I pull on my coat and fling myself on top of the snow and make a snow angel.

Enjoying the pure white.

I write my favourite names in huge letters in the yard so passing aircraft can read them.

I draw shapes with my footsteps and pummel the iron gate with snowballs. Just as I'm about to make a snowman, a parcel sails over the wall and lands in the yard.

It's from my neighbours.

And in it, is a hot cheese toastie. I have no idea how they have made it.

It is absolutely delicious.

They are being tried today on charges of 'inciting an uprising', because of a magazine cover they published. I thank them through the grate and wish them luck for the trial.

In the afternoon the news comes that they are to be released.

As they leave, I hear their footsteps echoing away in the corridor.

The recipe for **INMATE'S HOT TOASTIE** appears in their newspaper next morning:

ENSEMBLE: *Quarter a loaf of bread. Remove the inside and replace with the cheese. Wrap it in a carrier bag and place between the radiator bars overnight. Your hot toastie is ready in the morning.*

I smile. It is ingenious.

That night I make one for myself.

And I wake on the morning of New Year's Eve to a hot toastie cooked on the hearth that is my prison radiator. Waiting for me in its narrow slot, warmed through to the heart.

If life is the art of finding happiness in small things, prison is a masterclass.

It's deathly quiet today. But I'm determined to be cheerful.

The paper has announced that a New Year's party will be held at the prison gate that afternoon and that my wife and son will be there. I'm delighted by the thought that they'll be so close by. Maybe I'll hear them singing.

But the snowstorm outside turns into a blizzard. By the afternoon there are TV reports of a huge traffic accident involving more than thirty cars on the main route to the prison.

The lack of telephone or of any means of communication, is unbearable.

There's no more news. Nothing on any of the channels. No one tells me anything.

Tomorrow, I will discover that they are safe and well.

But tonight, for the first time, I believe that I am now completely alone.

CAN: Gul and I are placed in adjacent cells at first and
    forbidden from any contact. Then from time to time, we
    are allowed to meet while we take exercise under the
    constant gaze of the wardens.

    Other inmates can hold five – a-side matches. But because
    of the charges against us, all we are allowed to do is to
    kick and catch a ball between the two of us.

    Gul plays brilliantly – like the classy athlete he is, but I
    take all my rage out on the ball.

GUL: Anyone would think you're kicking somebody's head in.

CAN: The harder I kick, the higher the ball goes; I always
    end up kicking the ball up to the roof or into the overhead
    wires.

    These two distinguished newspaper editors then have
    to wait for the guards to fetch their ball back, like two
    downhearted kids.

CAN: Then, on 4 January, the warden comes in.

ENSEMBLE: 'I've got good news for you.'

CAN: Half an hour later Gul moves into my cell with all his
    belongings.

    To be honest we aren't all that close. We don't really
    know each other at all. And suddenly we're sharing every
    moment with each other. Gul seems to exist solely on
    books, newspapers and cigarettes. So many cigarettes. As
    soon as he arrives, he turns the nook under the stairs into
    a library.

    But Gul proves a true comrade. He is a journalist who's
    been living and breathing politics for years.
    We discuss the progress of our appeal – as it is rejected by
    each and every one of the courts across the land.

We have impassioned political debates, listen to music, sing songs when we get tired, and watch football together at the weekends.

But we have one single TV set and a single remote control.

At first we check to see what is being discussed on the panel debates in Gul's absence.

But I soon begin to try to distract him from it.

The moment any debate founders, I zap us towards a film. Sometimes even a reality TV show.

And he raises his head from his book, glances quizzically at this bizarre world of daytime television, and clicks his worry beads even faster.

Three weeks after Gul moves in with me, the charges against us brought by the government are finally confirmed.

CAN: 'It's fantastic!

GUL: 'They're seeking two life sentences for you, one aggravated. Plus a thirty-year sentence.'

CAN: 'Come on – if they'd said two years, I'd be worried, but multiple life sentences is ridiculous! It's a farce. They've got no evidence! We'll be out before you know it.'

Then on the 8th February our CEO brings good news;

CEO: 'The Constitutional Court has announced it will review your appeal.

The review date is set for 25th February.'

CAN: I am flying.
I start packing.

Gul isn't as thrilled as I am.

GUL: 'You don't know the pro-government media. There's trouble brewing around the progress of our case. Some plot will emerge to prevent our case being heard.

If the Constitutional Court reject our appeal, we'll never get out.'

CAN: I know he is right. The higher your hopes are, the harder the fall. But I think, what's the point of flying if you only hover just above the ground? Better to risk it and soar as high as you can.

CAN: There is no horizon in the cell. Just like our steps, our
    gaze comes up against a wall no matter which way we
    turn. Which is why every evening, before the guards
    come to remove from our sight the fading sky, its blue
    face paling, we gaze at that rectangle of sky long and hard,
    taking our fill... I know Spring will be the hardest part.
    Spring brings hope.

As the snow recedes, we swing wildly between believing we'll
be out any day now, and fearing we'll be in here forever.

The days start to grow longer, warmer, and the cynical
laughter of the crows is now accompanied by the first
chirps of the canaries.
The freshness of the buds popping outside floats in.
The first touch of spring on the yard pierces my heart.
Nature begins somersaulting in my blood.

The sun is now my calendar.
With each day it reaches further towards me, and I
convince myself we will be out by the time it comes down
the wall and fills the yard.

By the end of January, it creeps down to nearly two metres
above the iron door.
By early February, I'm able to stand on the chair and
touch it with my tired fingers. Like a father measuring his
child's height, I mark its position on the wall.
When I step onto the plastic chair on 13 February, I feel
sunlight on my face for the first time in months. It brushes
over my forehead and down to my chin.
As it starts to rise again ten minutes later, I reach up on
tiptoes to keep its touch on my skin for a little longer...
After it's gone, I'm glowing as if I've sunbathed for the
first time in my life

CAN: The rain never stops all through the night.

It lashes the roof.

At 7am, on 25th February, I wake with irrepressible hope inside.

It is the day of the Constitutional Court decision on our appeal.

The sun rises and finally it engulfs the yard.

Spring has come.

GUL: 'Unlawful! They've declared our detention unlawful.'

CAN: We will be released before we go to trial.
We hug.
We hop and skip like children.
Every channel runs the appeal verdicts at the same time.
The Warden comes in to congratulate us, adding the good news that we could be out of there within an hour of him receiving the order.
The hours drag like weeks.
We can see on TV our friends and family arriving outside the prison.
I want to remind everyone about all the journalists still inside and I want to thank our vigil keepers. They have shown that a wooden chair can overturn the will of a gilded throne.

At 2am the guards finally arrive; we load our stuff into a handcart. We call up the corridor to our neighbours:

'God save you,'

ENSEMBLE: 'Don't forget us,'

CAN: they call from their hatches.
We board a white van.
And are welcomed into the arms of our friends, families, and supporters, waiting at the prison gate.

CAN: The trial date is set for the 6th May.

The government is coming under increasing international pressure to protect freedom of speech and, as the case against us is being brought by the president himself, our fate is being talked about as a major test of democratic freedom. Finally, things are going our way. We begin to believe again that truth and reason will prevail.

On the morning of our trial the sun is out and I walk hand in hand with my wife to make my statement to the press on the steps of the court house:

'This is an attempt to arrest an entire profession, and with it, an entire nation. What we are seeing here is/'

(GUNMAN stands from a seat in the audience, raises a gun and fires at CAN.)

Gunshot.

Blackout.

(Exile. A pavement café in Berlin. Rain, evening. CAN enters and sits at the table under the awning in the rain. He takes out his notebook, and begins to write.)

CAN: **November 13th 2019** *(Insert today's date.)*

Dear Mr. President,

The weather here in Berlin is glorious.

I wish to extend my sincerest thanks for all you have done for my family and me.

Your relentless disregard for the rule of law has given us the rare privilege of appreciating just how many people care about us and the freedom of our country.

Thanks to my imprisonment you have allowed me a platform in the international media that most journalists can only dream of.

I must also thank you for paying such close attention to my wife, whose passport I understand is in your care. We greatly appreciate your protection following the attempt on my life, for which I also have you to thank.

(A brief moment of discomfort here, as CAN struggles with the instinct to look over his shoulder. He might take in the audience apprehensively.)

I look forward to greeting your assassins when they find me – however I understand from the local police that they have all been apprehended to date.

I look forward to the time when I will return to my homeland, embrace my wife and son, write freely and smile at the memory of these strange times.

(CAN may acknowledge the audience again on the last line.

He leaves.)

Blackout